# In Orbit

*For Nic and Arthur, always*

# In Orbit

## *Glyn Edwards*

Seren is the book imprint of
Poetry Wales Press Ltd.
Suite 6, 4 Derwen Road, Bridgend, Wales, CF31 1LH
www.serenbooks.com
facebook.com/SerenBooks
twitter@SerenBooks

ISBN: 978-1-78172-694-5
ebook: 978-1-78172-695-2

A CIP record for this title is available from the British Library.

The poems in this book are creative works by Glyn Edwards,
not a non-fiction account.

The publisher acknowledges the financial assistance of the Books Council of Wales.

Cover artwork: 'Disegni della Luna, novembre-dicembre 1609'
by Galileo Galilei, from the Biblioteca Nazionale di Firenze,
by kind permission of the Italian Ministry of Culture

Printed in Bembo by Severn, Gloucester.

# Contents

## One

## Two

## Three

*Remember, you cannot look at the sun or death for very long*
– David Hockney

One

# elegy

before beginning
please understand
there's no end here

in dark is dark
in night is night
in grief is grief

elegy is a book
the last page wrested
or left unwritten

all anyone can seek
to know is the time
to turn and come back

 alone

She rang to say you'd collapsed the night before at the snooker club in the village. I was marking exam papers on the sofa. The ambulance had been delayed, she said. You'd died on the way to the hospital, she said. Technically, or officially was the word she'd used – I can't recall which. I had started thinking of the balls left rolling on the table. And you, down on the floor, oblivious.

The fire exit doors were jammed. The paramedics struggled to get the stretcher out properly, she said. I saw your lean breath leave your mouth, charging the cold car park air. Your chest trembling like barbed wire in scant breeze. I looked away from the thought of you blue-lipped and half-dressed and dead as winter.

The family had followed the ambulance and had all waited outside the operating theatre. I imagined them ricocheting about the dimmed corridors, staring back at themselves in the midnight windows. They were all so unlucky, she said.

While she was quiet, I thought but did not say that most meteors heading for Earth burn up on entry to the atmosphere, where their threat shrinks to a distant streak of starlight, as sharp but as brief as a scratch from a cat. The comets we dread worse than cancer are the size of kidney stones when they're collected in the Outback, or the Steppe. I wanted to reassure her how close we come to our ending every day, every night. I could do nothing but imagine the snooker balls, all asteroids on a chart, following their infinite trajectories.

She began to cry. And then so did I. Then she stopped and I couldn't.

a single atom in an ion trap
headline a clipped page left
on a staffroom table above a
photograph of a pale blue dot
trapped between electrodes
barley two millimetres apart
suspended in an electric field
in a quiet Oxford laboratory
to create a direct and visceral bridge
between the quantum world
and macroscopic reality in the
frame of a digital camera held
at a vacuum chamber window
as blue-violet lasers illuminate
a strontium atom absorbing
and emitting their pale light
becoming visible to the eye

for weeks after they buried you
I picked blueschist off my shoes
rubbed it away from my fingers
never saw you crossing the yard
heard coughing from your room
noticed names change on doors
on the front of children's books
never thought death could be a
to any creation as divine as here
of that on a shelf quarried into
some silent strip of our universe
your omnipotence could form
again and find a way to share
a space with someone always
alone in an empty staffroom
finding blue flecks on floor tiles
sitting beside your empty seat

# Antipodes

We are waiting in your shrunken classroom,
warming our wet shoes on the growling pipes
below the windowsill, drawing cocks in the condensation

until you come in, later than usual, shake yourself dry
like a damp dog and stare at a computer screen.
*Did you hear about the earthquake, Sir?*

You nod, though your eyes don't nod. *The tremors,*
says a voice, desperate to rescue you, *set off car alarms*
*in London – the other side of the world.* You are silent,

so close now to the monitor that when you stir
it's as if you're butting your forehead against the glass.
You are wearing yesterday's clothes. Slowly, you stand

and unpin two huge maps from the display boards,
deliberately, like a general collapsing a failed campaign.
You line up one upon the other as a bedsheet on a mattress

folding the countries like bodies, so that the arm of America
holds the waist of India, so the Atlantic bathes Australia.
*They're not diametrically opposite*, your voice is all wrong.

*If we went down, down, through the centre of the world,*
*we'd surface and sink somewhere in the Pacific.*
You're searching the stunned space for something

and clench at a shining metal from the desk.
You gauge the maps again, lift them like a flag
and stab them through with the shaft of a pen.

Soon, you are shuffling across the yard in the rain,
your coat still on your chair. We take the maps away.
Your fountain pen is splintered. Your computer screen blank.

Daylight Saving. The clocks went back last night but the boy next door has forgotten. His alarm springs forward from his room and falls back into mine. Through the wall I hear drawers and doors and I count one, two, three, four stairs and then it is silent again. Dawn is yet to fuss at the curtains. The boy must be downstairs now, fiddling to switch on a lamp, putting on trainers, tucking jeans into socks so they don't catch in the teeth of the bikechain. He'll exist briefly under streetlights. When he gets to the newsagents, he'll find an endless dark behind the glass and he'll wait there until the new day begins.

The blackness of the room has no depth: I could be staring at the ceiling, or at the floor. But neither of these shades are your black – you are beyond black now. I won't rise until there's light enough that I must. I cannot sleep. Instead, I am staring at my eyelids and I'm a boy again, and I'm delivering papers on the round I held for years. I'm struggling again to swing the weight of the Sundays over my awkward shoulders. I can't balance my racing bike on the sheer fences, can't force the magazines through the taciturn letterboxes. I'm looking through endless single paned windows at the darkness indoors; my silhouette is a frost thawing on the glass.

I begged my dad to do the shift so I could go on your school camping trip and look at the stars. Dad refused to even discuss it and, then, relented quite suddenly, like a roof giving way quietly days after the rain has stopped. He must have remembered he'd be leaving us soon anyway.

It was late October, damp. The heating in the minibus hadn't been fixed. The back doors were hinged shut with rope to keep the dozen rucksacks from tumbling out like cadavers. We were warned that the camp-fire wouldn't light easily, so we stopped and had chips somewhere with a grey castle and a grey quay. Everyone chewed their regrets doggedly: the cold, the sudden gloom, the smoky clouds; the group numbed in the silence. Perhaps that was why teachers changed the camp site they'd first mapped out; maybe they too were disorientated by the thickness of the dark.

We were on a rutted lane, high hedges like hands at the van's windows, docile behind the brake lights of a wagon that hesitated at each shadow and bend. That lane could have hugged the whole county because for hours I saw the same two strips of red glowing more abruptly, and heard wheels growl and churn, the suspension groan, the railings jar and something metal roll upon metal. When the truck eventually turned, the teacher must have slowed in relief and the minibus stalled. Our eyes trailed the truck as it stumbled noisily into shadow, the flatbed empty as an open mouth.

We stammered slowly out of the black valley, put our tents up in pairs and felt dew settling on their skins instantly. You were assembling telescopes but lapsed to stare at the stars: *The whole hemisphere is here; the entire northern hemisphere.*

You shaped our eyes at The Northern Cross, and urged us to ignore the truck still banging down the hidden lanes.

*There'll be peace soon enough, boys. Have patience.*

But the jackhammer of axel against dirt was now a regular workshop thrum, driven by pulse upon anvil. A steady mass being struck in forge. And your belief was extinguished too.

*Even Hephaestus made less noise than that fucking vehicle.*

You began to collapse the telescopes – you knew first – and we followed your focus to fresher noises amongst the metals. A single cow was lowing but the plaintive noise was sped up, hurried, like it was forcing itself out of her the way grief does. And then, more cows began to stamp their resistance at the loading ramp, sobbing, thrashing against the horizontal bars. More and more cows mourning breathlessly at the truck's maw.

*We'll go as soon as there's light. As soon as there's light.*

I lay in my sleeping bag fully clothed. My hat pulled over my ears, my hood raised. The boy from the year above had his eyes open whenever I checked. We said nothing. It was cold enough for the stars to lean right out of the anthracite night and press down upon the tent roof as stalagmites. Cold enough for my breath to condense as nebula.

Someone in another tent was crying. Your voice tried to soothe them, *One more hour.*

So we counted and waited and the constellations faded into the lining of the tent. You had made a fire and were stirring a pot of porridge. When the ladle clashed at its edge, you shuddered and apologised. The ringing noise was still there – tinnitus, or a bird mimicking the echoes of hoof on metal. We were driven down the hills. You were in the passenger seat, trying to update the digital clock, the minibus awkwardly navigating the mud ricked up by reluctant wheels. We slowed at every junction and my dread of the cows made them half-there, dim and shapeless behind the bars, their eyes heavy doused lamps.

*As soon as there's light.*

There is no one near me this morning to half the solitude. Nobody to dilute the night. The paperboy's bike slips from the alleyway. It sounds like a watch's second hand stumbling to find its rhythm. Somewhere down the street, a car's ignition coughs in the cold.

I stare upwards and search for your voice. As soon as there's light. It's a slender star to seek but the quickest way to lose a black hour.

# Tombolo

We stand with the wind with the dunes with the Atlantic
without you. A teacher from the other class drove the schoolbus here
so the field trip could continue. She hands out clipboards thick
with graffiti and worksheets on grid surveys, tells us to persevere.

You'd told us about a naturalist who'd collected toads each night
for a week along the thinning Formby coast to release
them in Talacre, taxiing them to the edge of their earth in his boot,
his glovebox. Until his back seats looked lined with verdigris.

When we tell her, she says never heard of the natterjack.
It isn't her fault that she isn't you. She is kind, has twins
in Year Seven, takes time to learn our names, to understand, asks
us about next year's plans. We ask her if she's spoken to you.

She shakes her head, a colleague saw you at the fireworks stand
in the new supermarket staring up at the display.
She stops, looks around. *That lighthouse there is almost an island.*
*It's tied to these dunes by the thinnest thread of sand*, says

*It's called a tombolo.* Repeats it, points at a question on the sheet.
In pairs we turn and fill in the forms about erosion, make up
the results of a study on grasses. I search for toads half-heartedly.
*Sometimes the beach fortifies itself*, the teacher's voice interrupts

*but often the tie erodes and the island drifts off the maps entirely.*
At hometime, I find her: Did they say anything to you by the fireworks?
*Yes:* she replies, she did try, you just talked quietly
about the bad weather, the rockets unlit in their boxes.

# Cofiwch Dryweryn

You swear you can't remember it swollen so high,
so we balance at your wet window on tall stools
like chess pieces, calculating the river's rise
and counting down to when its banks will break. All rules
revised, we start to drum and pound upon the glass:
*ten, nine, eight, seven, six, five, four, three,* hysterically
we chant, daring the day to deny our trespass,
but the fields and farms we've forged into our grid city
withstand. We descend from our nests to the classroom,
stills of subdued Tryweryn are on the board now:
its graveyards underwater, a church spire that is
lifting its head at low tide, families dredged from their homes
as water urges in at the speed of life. *How
are we elevated by the sinking of villages?*

*not his*
*home,*
*Japan,*
*but a*
*home*
*from*
*home*
*of sorts*
*during*
*WW2*
*where,*
*as the*
*sole*
*survivor*

*he was*
*kindled*
*in fire*
*during*
*an air*
*raid*
*over an*
*island*
*in the*
*South*
*Pacific*

*after*
*his unit*
*died*
*from*
*fatal*
*wounds*
*from*
*hunger*
*from*
*disease,*
*he was*
*ordered*
*to die too,*

*when*
*he had*
*no left*
*arm to*
*draw*
*with*
*and he*
*began*
*to use*
*his right*

Now that the strip of manga comics masked all the blown plasterwork above the blackboard, you could have stood anywhere really. But, this time, for this girl, you stop below the poster you'd begun with and point out the details: the skeleton looming green a cartoon boy being chased down a stark riverbank.

    The new girl sits beside me, draws her arm from the makeshift sling the school nurse tied at break, rests the white bandage on the blue desk. Her fingertips are tiny heads vanishing into a creased hand. The tired letters come together like a writing in caricature. She senses your shape fixed behind us.

*there*
*is no*
*excuse*
*Shigeru*
*Mizuki*
*said*
*long*
*after*

    *I don't want to use my wrong hand.*

    It's only the second thing she has said to you today. You lean on the back of her chair, your wedding ring tapping the black plastic.

    *When we are learning, we just delight in every mark we can make.*

    She holds the pen as still as she can. It squirms like a child's crayon in her right hand as she draws around her left.

# wish fulfilment as montage

The camera follows a note as it's passed.
There's a close up of a hand in shirt cuffs, shoulder taps.

The paper is folded tight as tourniquet; a neat suture
within lists name, location, time, question mark.

One waits, staring up at leaves, brave in May-light,
the other climbs the lane as shadow might, uncertainly,

but their charged hands draw and repel while they walk –
their arms poles, their fingers loosened by magnetism.

They wade the riveredge, the open-mouthed culverts,
and explore until their reflections are licked clean

by grey water. Behind the graves buried in the woods
dimorphic yews are skirted in fruit, there they undress

seeds by the handful and deposit all that red flesh
shamelessly at the moondoors to the badger sett.

They throw rocks at the old brickworks as they pass,
wait as glass folds back and breaks again in the dark.

One grows their hair, one crops theirs to skull stubble;
they appear to be the same pasture on different days.

Fast forward boys become men and sex is shown as shirt
buttons shelled like berries, dusk-pricked skin, a pen sketch

of a torso, bedsheets. Now, their car is slow through
a city steepled in skyline, lecture halls, pubs and parks

and again in piano shelf photos: a wedding slow dance, a dog,
a terrace garden up to its waist in snow, kids in uniform.

The camera need only imply, so when it fades to black,
to curtains barely reopening, it connotes the end is near.

One stares from a window, their back to the world, the other
offers tissues folded to a dense pad. When one looks down,

they notice the name on it isn't theirs. That it never was.
They reach out, tap a shoulder. The camera follows the note.

just as blood makes
bones makes blood
makes bones makes
blood you make me

just as rock unmakes
rock time unmakes
time seasons unmake
seasons you unmake me

# The Moon as a Drone

They are walking home across the bridge,
the rods banging against wet legs.
and stop to find the places below
that they'd fished all day when one says
*it's those you lose that you most remember*
or something like that.
                    One of them points out
how the tree crowns are wary of each other
on the river islands below, all mustard yellow,
before shy leaves drop. They're trading dialects
*skerries aits cays islets ayots keys holms*
                    and clouds course the water.

A figure is dropping something – paper, rubbish –
and thinking about the men roped together
that climbed the rail last week and fell,
hitting the pier structure or the rocks below.
Your silence is falling from that same height,
and washing up at my feet.
                    Along the riverbank
two women are taking turns to pilot their drone –
a homing pigeon writing messages on the wing.
Its bird's eye seeing swans as single feathers,
waders as floating seed and distance will grind
                    a rocky shore to fine sand.

*Like the spores below fern fronds*
a lecturer will say when the film is viewed
*or yeast cells growing in petri-dishes.*
All concentration is drawn to the islands
instead of the river's swell. Even the moon
is distracted by itself in water.
                    I approach the undertow
where the water eddies before the bridge
But, waist high in the anonymous dark, I stop,
look down: there are so many stars carried
upon the river's surface it seems like the sky
is breaking. I slip the stones from my pockets.

# River

a river is mirror is poem
parsing truth from whatever
light you allow yourself seen in

a mirror is poem is river
hurrying in its promise
to devour all it distorts

a poem is river is mirror
held to your own mouth
to check you're still breathing

# A photocopy sellotaped to a desk
## – *Picking Flowers* by Henri Lebasque

We begin copying them anyway-
these images we discovered,
    without cultivating or caring for.

                It is easiest just to sketch them
                        than acknowledge the teacher,
                his grey eyes chronic below coins.

        *He had a breakdown before,* a voice says
    *began painting red on his forearms,*
        *red over his hands, red on the table.*

                But today, for the substitute teacher,
                        he has just stuck printouts on desks,
                and walked out and it has snowed briefly.

        The printer's saturated all the paintings
    so colour, season, youth, meaning
        are muted, though two women wait

                in a lane and stare at the same white bird
                        as the painter did, as I do – all four of us,
                simultaneously, urging its stillness.

        *So, what does the bird represent then?*
    Now, suddenly, five of us. I expect
        the startled bird to fly at your intrusion

                (though you are never an intrusion)
                        and I don't need to turn to find your voice
                *Why are the women's faces obscured?*

        I release the bird by looking beyond it
    to the women, their patterned dresses
        identical as the lush verges, their faces

                clouded, shadowed, and I say, or you say,
                        or we announce, simultaneously,
                *one figure is conjuring the other.*

The day had turned a hard dark without me noticing. The few lonely stars seemed surprised by the shorter evenings and were too conspicuous suddenly.

Earlier, I'd bought a card from the newsagents opposite the school. I half-hid it like a porno in the folds of a newspaper and, once I'd smuggled it home, I sat in front of its emptiness for an hour.

I had no right to hold my grief. And there was no way I could map or track it.

I'd wanted to write to you for decades. When I was your student, I followed my feelings to your classroom once. Knowing the building was empty and seeing your light still on, I found you there, the walls naked around you. You had stripped the displays and looked as if you had forgotten how to dress them again. We decorated the space together and drank tea and I couldn't share what was troubling me and you explained that finding an analogy can be the clearest way to discern something difficult.

In the summer before I left for university, I wrote to you about ellipses: how the same word is shared by the pathways objects make in orbit and the grammatical mark for omission. At the end of the card I drew three circles and signed my name. I imagined how you must have shied at the card because really you'd never needed the sleight of hand analogy anyway. How you'd probably slip it back into the envelope and bury it beneath the clutter in your desk drawer or stack it amongst a tower of bedside books. How it'd grow there like ivy or illness until it covered your journal, your possessions, your skin, your voice.

Perhaps the postcards you sent were simply postcards, nothing more, but I would study them until their pictures were analogies, until the stars were clear on the murmurating birds, until the butterflies became migrating Monarchs, until all the words meant more at night.

When we worked with each other, every routine was an ellipse of sorts: lunchtimes beside you; parent's evenings on adjacent desks; the way we looped our cars after saying goodbye. And every pause was an omission of something that had taken too long to voice.

*Thinking of you in these difficult times …*

27

Two

There's no king of Bardsey Island anymore but there were regents of sorts a hundred years ago and their dynasties were lobster pots, ruined chapels and island exodus.

In the museum display there are three monochromes of the island's lineage: two kings, that seem dragged by winds in their photographs, are slumped gaunt as gallows below their crowns. Then there is one body that wears the home-made coronet the way the sea wears light. The stark sky behind him could be kindled by storm or summer, and the boats on the beach may be shivering in cold sand or warm still from the sea – so much of this picture is ambiguous – but the man's pride is as clear as his crown and all the saturated greys grow as gold as fish scales.

The pictures and the crown seem so familiar though I can recall little of the rest of the displays. The museum felt bigger somehow, the city smaller. Perhaps the coach driver stopped here for his lunch after a visit to the slate mines, or you guided the class this way when a trip to the pier was interrupted by rain. I remember you telling the group we must discover an artefact each so we could share what we'd found on the bus back to school, but that journey is a fogged window now. I walk about the other exhibits and try to recall other people's treasures. I drink coffee in the quiet cafe, and, before I leave, I return to the display.

What I found during your lessons, I pressed to myself. Even then I knew. I would have worn you that way if you had let me. I would have taken the moods your wife seemed to suffer like a heavy sky, taken the crude angles you made of your hands and your lips and I would have worn you weightlessly.

I would have worn you like this broken king wore his tin crown.

Instead, I would look at Venus through my telescope and see the platinum glare before the rest of the night sky manifest itself to distracted streetlamps and tight-drawn curtains

I would
pretend it was a shared sight.
Each evening, of all the lighted worlds our
eyes could inhabit, we'd draw our gaze to the same
one. You had other stars to study first; washing dishes in
lukewarm water, shirtsleeves rolled; reading to kids too young to
remember you; ironing your lessons; fucking your wife, or showering
her away. All points of reference that could have you led anywhere, but
you'd search out Venus too. Not your first star – not a star at all you'd say – but
argent, profound.

When you asked the class which planet was closest to the sun, I bit my lips hard.
*Mars.*
You looked away to another hand.
*Earth.*
*The moon.*
*Venus. And it shines so brightly because it reflects so much of the sun's rays.*
And once you'd let them study the other lights first, you found me and I radiated.
Mercury is closest. Venus is next and it doesn't shine. Its glare comes from a band of
gasses that permits radiation to enter its atmosphere but refuses to let the heat
escape.
The group gathered as you sketched a whiteboard diagram. Someone joked how it
looked like a trampled Valentine. Arrows entering and entering and the heart
swelling red and red and red and dead.
*Venus is cooking itself.*

I'd drawn stars in pupils' books once. Now, marking is staring at a
clouded sky and waiting for it to pass. When I hear the
radiatiors' tired breaths or the final beat of next door's
back gate, I count the quiet houses one by
one and, in the enchanting dark, I
look at Venus

# Parallel Circuit

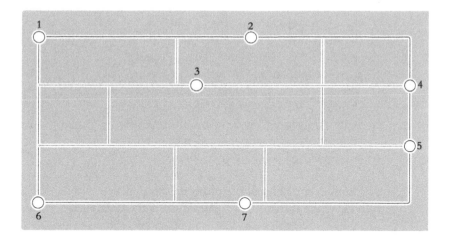

1 when I listened carefully, there was always coughing, and always a bell ringing. It had rung minutes ago and the corridors had filled many minutes ago. The corridors had cleared minutes ago and when I listened carefully, I heard the coughing and heard the bell and

2 you were standing in the corridor between two closed doors. You stood like you'd been told to wait there. You stood like you'd always been there. Fused in that place, looking levelly at the wall, your head fully framed by

3 a poster I half-remembered seeing elsewhere in the school. There was a factory glowing in it, and tower blocks alive in the blue dark. I remembered it more and found again a lit road coiling round a coastline, quiet docks, different textures to the water – an estuary emptied of tide, a midnight train readying to depart perhaps

4 *It's a mainframe,* your voice charged and certain – *from a computer, or something more modern. Like a server.*
*Not a satellite photograph?* I said, stepping forward – so we stood parallel to the poster – and you resisted:

5 *it is – but we're the satellites – we're the lens – and we're looking down on whatever circuitboard city we want to construct.* We considered which capacitor should be your office, and the transistors that would become schools and hospitals and churches. *If the city was always dressed in black – would living feel like mourning?* And the next day

6 we would plan new paths that wired through the park and could walk along the beach until the sea came and its current threatened to

7 disconnect us. In the morning, I stood fused in front of the poster's urban twilight. I heard a bell ringing and the corridors filled. The corridors emptied and I listened carefully.

# Moon phases as seen from Earth

There are crescent moons forming
up my fingernails and crescent moons
bitten at their end. The bare light bulb
is a full moon. Briefly, the flaring cigarette
become a full moon. When I stare through
the new moon at a bottle's top like it's a telescope,
I find another new moon. Last night, a storm
bent the oaks into waxing moons and now
there's too many moon seeds at their roots to mass
into polished handfuls of moon rock.

Boys kick a full moon around the car park.
There is a quarter moon curvature to the unlit lane
where memories pass like waning moons
of an argument, when mouths were gibbous moons
with malice. A busker now has a new moon
in the middle of his guitar and the new moon
at his feet is half-filled by full moons. His black dog
has two moons behind clouds for eyes. I cover
my face to hide the cold moons on my cheeks.

Moons catseye the carriageway below me
and full moons are fastened to the front of cars.
The rain is making moons at my feet.
Every distubed puddle is a moon phase.
*The moon is so-called as it measured months.*
*moon, mona, metri, mensis* – you made us chant it,
made us discover moons everywhere. A person jumps
from this crescent moon bridge every month.
Six moons have passed since you died.

I put on my shirt, my tie. I stepped into my trousers. I sat on the bed's edge to fix my shoelaces. I moved to the window.

*I won't be in today. My mother has taken a turn. For the worse. I won't be able to send my lessons in now. I have to go back to the hospital. Right now. I am. Sorry.*

The phone illuminated as it reconnected with the charger. A man in the road looked up at my window. He had moved in last year, or the year before. I lifted an arm. He nodded, twice, then turned away. He was on the phone too, his back against his little car, bags on the floor beside him. I wanted to ask him if he needed help. I wanted him to ask.

On the news, the shadow cabinet talked about the costs of living. I tried to work out if the city behind the studio window was a still. When the boat lights interrupted the river, I switched off.

I walked to the supermarket to find what I needed. Each aisle had a large cage filled with flattened boxes and a lady my mother's age made the same joke to everyone who squeezed past.

*A little boy could have made a great fort from all of these.*

Most of the long tables in the coffee shop were taken: a mother's group code switched Welsh and English - a car driving into and away from radio signal; students with earphones in swiping between screens; commuters drinking while checking watches, drinking while checking phones.

The newspaper I found was a week out of date. Scientists had discovered a way to check if Shrodinger's cat was alive or dead without having to look.

On the table beside me, a lady adjusted her hijab. She was looking down, remembering. Her starling blue-black veil framed her concentration like a portrait. She was speaking quietly to another lady who was making bullet point notes on a jotter pad.

All we ever really do is try to solve our problems in other people's lives.

The news article wouldn't make sense for me. The paradox of not looking and not knowing had been overcome by the notion of taking a picture in the dark. Somehow, every photon of light transfers energy to and from the object in view. I rubbed my eyes. My tea had stewed a thick brown.

I looked up and the lady was smiling at me, her face made into a thin moon by the silk.

*Your shoelaces are undone.*

I read the article again and again until it made sense. I walked home. I wondered how anyone could tolerate allowing life to become death, how anyone could condone even a hypothetical light to dim in a box.

# Sun, Earth and Moon scale model
# (Oxford Natural History Museum)

To stand together by the gallery
pillars looking down at Anning's
ichthyosaur, at a triceratops skull.
To imagine the air as a dense strata
filled with fossils. To notice then
two pinheads in a display case
and an explanation of scale beyond

comprehension. To hear you count
all nine zeros and read aloud that
there is a third sphere across the hall
the equivalent size and distance
of the sun. To see how you first flinch
then stare at the gilded ball and to know
what you will ask next. To tell you

*there's one billion seconds in a decade*
and to watch you translate our lives
into time, and to watch you transpose
time into distance, and to watch you lean
so close to the glass that your head
eclipses the painted earth, and its tiny,
textured moon, and to watch you.

# Aesop's Crow

As crow
made water rise
up a clear jug
on a bone dry day,
so shall I stir you
to your surface
with wintry pebbles.

I'll leave them
below the dashboard
between blown fuses,
on a key seized in a lock
like a trapped voice,
in sick days,
in blank essays.

You will fill yourself
with sincere stares,
thank you cards,
that bottle of whiskey
on the bottom shelf,
with books, with stars,
with pebbles.

## 'nocturnal'

suppose I take
      the word 'nocturnal'
            make it my home

     curl up within it
         the way a fox does days
              while the world is oblivious

         write it white on black
            fold it in an envelope
               post it to your pocket

           where you can let it sleep
             or open it half the day
                and meet me there

# Hunter's Moon

the new neighbours
are burning leaves
in a metal drum

        bonfire stink
        soaks shadows
        on the clothes

                I clip them
                from the line
                in clogged twilight

you'd put a link
on the class forum
about moon phases

          through sinking smoke
          through night cloud
          my sister's sleepless tears

                  I fold tomorrow's uniforms
                  looking up trying
                  to see what you see

I write back
on the computer
saying thanks

        for the reminder
        sit for an hour to see
        the message collected

                the morning is cold clear
                no smoke no cloud
                no message no moon

# Smoots or

meuses, sometimes smeuses,
  fox lines between hedges
    a badger track below a fence,

a gate forced by horses
  that's storm swung for weeks
    and shrugged its hinges.

the wintry ground within
  that hoof-churned glade
    has quietly gone to dust.

oaks widening wooden rings
  so the light they let past
    is thin as gas on the floor

where celandine trails
  to sun-warm limestones
    dredged up, cairned, moss-soft.

quartz veins, fossils
  of stems in cross-section.
    a spider's thread, solitary bees.

nettles outgrow the mound
  stems purpled, veined,
    leaf hands seizing space.

# Paternity Leave

With you not about
    I found this van left
        so far on the curb
midway down the street
    that I made a test
        to inch round her curves
without touching it
    pretending it best
        she stayed undisturbed

    so solitary
        and piebald in rust
            this lonely dragon
    that each morning I
        began brushing past
            stroking her patterns
saw her lean and lie
    in graffitied dust
        and traffic warnings

    on New Year's Day
        the abandoned van
            was chained to a truck
led away like a condemned
    horse by a man who would not
        listen, his shotgun cocked
out the neighbours came
    to their yards and drank
        I wanted to sink

        in the same way
       the pavement had sunk
    below familiar bulk

# Stargazing

quarry one, two, three
lights from the slate sky
and we feel Earth curve
beneath precarious feet
 before eyes calibrate
 quicker than cognition
 and the hundred stars
 are beyond our tongue
  then alien to all numbers
  a thick night without depth
  time suddenly unwinding
  so wildly we step indoors
   where gravity can be seized
   and the sole celestial body
   fast behind the slate glass
   is just oneself reflected back

# Blackbird

There was no way I could have stopped of course,
my car rolling towards the junction
the dashboard clock already past the hour

but there was something in the force
of the traffic lifting your feathers
closer and closer to the wheels

that made me turn into a narrow street
I'd not noticed before, leave the orange eyes blinking,
and run back to where I'd abandoned you,

wrap you in a suit jacket or a coat,
rest you in a shoebox or schoolbag
so you didn't ricochet around the boot

and transform you with time and mistruth
to a heartsore crow in a prisoner's pocket
where we'd wing it together – shoelace jesses, idle nests –

practice flights dusted onto windows,
neither of us fearing how deep a beak could sink,
and only this poem as single cage

to return to and descend in the same shock
that a bird's body has barely any weight
yet yours was so heavy in empty hands.

The bells in their gables were stilled, the stars on the ceiling were subdued, sad. I sat in the front pews, with the older teachers who'd shared decades with you. The science technician beside me said you'd pulled her ponytail when you were in primary school together. The family were balled up at by the stage, sobbing. A row of rounded backs.

*I've seldom seen the hall so filled,* began the vicar and the congregation turned as a single corvid mass, suddenly aware of one another. There were so many faces I knew. Staff who'd retired or moved on, former pupils I half-recognised but whose memories were different shapes. Then there were the current students, sad-smiling, checking their watches, teachers picking dog hairs from funeral coats, the headmistress at her phone. And they all brushed up on to the plinth, tapped the microphone one, two times and shared sturdy stories: a brother nearly drowning in a swollen pond, a young man on a dig in Egypt, losing a whole class in a gallery, falling asleep in meetings and at the club, forgetting anniversaries, remembering telephone numbers, forgetting which side of the road to drive on, remembering to feed the fish, forgetting, remembering. Forgetting.

When a casket is sealed, people are content to touch a corner of the coffin as they leave. When it is kept open, the final act of remembering demands the closer study of death. People slowed down, but didn't stop. As they glanced at and quickly away from the corpse, a queue gathered. I waited. I thought how long it would take for the wood and the wool and the skin and the skeleton to be forgotten in the oven and I thought you would approve of being atomised. I thought perhaps your becoming part of something huge and heavy and close and distant would have reassured you while the lights in your brain became black.

But when I looked into the coffin, I stopped and I studied you. I was wrong. Nothing would have reassured you in death for your face had slipped sideways from its skull and the left eye was whiter and wider, and your left cheek had lurched and the nostrils were taut and your lips were lost in palsy.

Three

The headmistress' PA had left a voicemail every day last week. Her voice was traffic noise, half hidden by windy oaks on some faraway road.

Today's voice was a different vehicle: all black, a curved cat's back, windows like switched off tv screens, an unspeaking silhouette for a driver. It was phlegmatic; a reading of rehearsed words while she scrolled down a HR document, *period of leave…concern for well-being…attendance policy…matter of urgency.*

This morning's voice belonged to the Headteacher and it may as well have said, *get in the back, don't make a fuss.*

At school, the caretaker was crouched in the porchway, collecting tiny oak leaves into his hand. When the reception doors slid open, he sighed and regathered the fallen leaves. I waited in the lobby and feigned interest at the pupils' artwork on the display boards. The same fireworks sketches revived by new chalks. When the receptionist returned to her post at the desk, she smiled over her coffee and pressed the button concealed under her counter. Moments later, the Headmistress swept in.

I had intended to tell the truth: that I'd been absent through mourning; that it was grief that stilled the phone in my hand when I tried to call. But, in the open office, in front of her closed face, I emptied myself of lies instead. I said my mother had stage three cancer and was undergoing intensive radiography. I fumbled over the first words that came to mind and tried them all like they were keys to someone else's house, *period…concern… policy…urgency.*

She said she was upset I felt I couldn't let the school know. Particularly at such a sad time for the school. She said I should return by next week. That she wished my mother's treatment success. When I tried to shake her hand, I caught her fingers instead and she withdrew them. I shuffled away, and thought of my mother sunbathing in Malta, her grandchildren burning about the pool.

It rained and rained and the bonfire in the park was cancelled.

Dogs howled down the street all evening. The muted fireworks from across the valley sounded like a stranger thudding at a thick door that wouldn't open.

# A photo of the moon shows not a moon but a moon being looked at

From the craters on the pink moon, we plot a familiar face,
and out of its disk, we fashion a sphere – our vicarious Earth.
But we're deceived, for each night seven billion moons occur –
a lantern for each one of us, a momentary memory trace.

*Have you ever done the experiment on impact craters?*
Mum had sent me back to school the day after dad died,
and someone had asked you to comfort me so you'd laid
equipment out in advance: chair; tissues; a glass of water.

*Yes, we went to the beach, collected pebbles and rocks*
*dropped them on sand, varied the angles, the velocity –*
*the more violent the impact was, the greater the cavity.*
You were measuring empty spaces too. *It doesn't stop*

you said, *that experiment – it should not conclude on loss.*
Instead, if we had watched the tide return to gently level
the sand, we'd remember how craters on Earth are filled,
*how the moon alone has its history written across its face.*

You circled the tea in your mug, looked out the window
and explained how tectonics sift the planet's surface
so loss is recycled into life. *While the dusty footprints*
*of astronauts are still on the moon, here there's growth.*

And I kept your counsel as my atmosphere, until your death
when there was no impact crater anyone could measure.
*There are collapsed volcanoes on the moon – caldera –*
*and at certain times in the year, you'll be able to see them.*

All day the sky had been lucid. By dusk, the moon is pink
but its promised perigee is bleached behind clouds
and I am at the bathroom mirror not beside your words.
I switch off the lights until I am just a grey in all this dark.

| **Orange Death** | **Sparkle Dun** |
|---|---|
| Blue Winged Olive | Rusty Spinner |
| Gold Ribbed Hare's Ear | Zonker |
| Lefty's Deceiver | Mrs Simpson |
| Muddler Minnow | Red Setter |
| Orange Death | Sparkle Dun |
| Royal Wulff | Elk Hair Cadder |
| Black Ghost | Copper John |

The list slipped from a book
    I'd not looked at for a decade
        – little changes more in a person
            than how they hide in handwriting –

                I didn't recognise it to begin with
                  thought the words a taxonomy
                    of moths maybe, wildflowers
                      aliases, Gold Cup winners
until I checked on the computer
    saw angling flies, fishing lures
        and quickly all the other things
            I'd not noted down resurfaced:
                borrowing a book from your shelf
                  just so I could ask you questions
                    you knowing it just subterfuge
                      but still trying to answer them

# おもひでぽろぽろ
*(Only Yesterday)*

*Back to being a child again, leaning at a window,*
*waiting for the giant figure in the hillside to stir.*
*Somehow, as I age in the dream, so he grows*
*until he inhabits the landscape entirely one night*
*and I urge him to hoist his wooded head free,*
*to haul up his limestone skeleton, to look at me.*

When the dream appeared so flush on my lips
I told you it breathlessly, interrupting myself,
impolite, forgetful in my keenness to revisit it.
And I saw your eyes were looking beyond me,
the clock or the door, wishing I were silent.
I gauged the dream, and you, were fantasy.

Vicissitude was animated in that pineapple
the family saw as too sacrosanct to open
one night, too monotonous to chew the next.
Except, in the Studio Ghibli film, the schoolgirl
summoned her stubbornness, and refused
to abandon her bowl, her event, until sated,

when, in reality, there was always a moment
intrigue relented into indifference; and this was it.
This was the stray dog my uncle gave as a gift
one Christmas that we stroked, played with,
loved, and ignored until it ran away from us –
until we allowed it to run away. As I turned to go,

you drew yourself upright in the chair so slowly
it creaked like roots being unwound, and reached
an arm for my shoulder. Standing close enough
then to be warmth on glass, you said, *I think that*
*when we place ourselves in windows in dreams,*
*we always do so as much to see as to be seen.*

# Imitation

For a year or two, perhaps more, parents daubed bedsheets
with children's names, hung them here at the front of the estate
like communal washing between trees as aide-memoire
for 16ths, 18ths. When the anniversaries lapsed, the weather
would untie them, fold them in leaves, tuck them away
from sight.
       Nobody is out there now to flag up birthdays –
maybe councilmen cut them down in cold mornings, or families
forget. But the oaks keep mementos: cached in their canopies,
like loosened Xmas decorations, are countless cotton strings;
spry pockets pit the trunk where bungees knotted; half-rings
faint as c-section scars when ropes clamped to the bark.

Last night, I left the bus a stop too soon to walk the early dark
between the trees and remember how I begged my mum
not to announce my birthday on a sheet there, and how numb


       I was when she forget the day completely. Throwing sticks
          to unsettle conkers was my neighbour's youngest,
     a line of anime game cards laid out in a tarot prediction

    at her feet. She began turning them over, face up, face down.
          *They're fake – look at them – I swapped them yesterday*
  *and I was happy. They could be real.* Still knelt on the ground,  she
    described how others laughed when they'd explained the lie,
        and throughout she'd turned the cards. Hating. Loving.
      *Can't you just pretend they're real?* My words magnify
    the betrayal. *They're fake. Everyone knows. And now I know.*

    I gathered up the game as she left, took it home, scrutinised it:
       no flaws, no trick to reveal the cards weren't authentic, no
  answer as I returned them. I left them in a thick pile by the door.
  Amid trees, tomorrow night, a papery snow will scatter the floor.

# If God is a black hole

                              six million billion miles away
then knees bridged beside a bed
                              elbows sunk into its thin duvet
perfect hands squared in prayer
                              pleading proof of parental love

is no different a little lifetime later
                              to kneeling on a stranger's floor
fingers clamped around a thigh
                              a palm opened as if below a book
steadying the mass as it grows
                              pleading proof of provisional love.

For while things forced together
                              exert such pressure as they meet
that they create something new –
                              maybe memories, maybe mountains –
both black holes Gods withhold
                              their atoms, light, their proof of life.

# Bird Drawings by CF Tunnicliffe

For a stunned second
after it struck the window
the starling fanned its wings
then folded and fell away,
the glass rattling its casement
like a brittle-boned body.

The startled class are stilled
around the sill as the bird stirs,
labours off into the treeline –
its dusty night-sky primaries
collected on the glazing
in a feather map nebulae.

*A Shame,* I start to say,
*if it had lulled from the ledge, we could have gathered the*
*carcass from the yard, bought it upstairs to draw* and study it.
Scale it. I show them photographs of Tunnicliffe in his
Technician's coat, gloveless hands unfolding the
wave-wide feathers of a fulmar and mapping them like
planets on an easel as endless as an astronomer's chart:
converts to comets, scapulars to satellites, fingers fore
and ring pivoting in pairs of compasses, plotting the
albatross anatomy like a universe of atoms. But to the
class every dead bird is a dodo so I open the door, let
them quietly fledge before the lesson bell sounds.

& when                One boy has stayed back and stands the board his
he unpacks the        gaze as gripped as a red rosehead pinioned in a
broken crow from his  flowerpress, his breaths barely beating.
old rucksack its snapped
neck cracks against a desk & oilspill                 *Lean closer,* I urge. *Until*
black clots into inked wings, waxed eyes,             *your mourning makes it fly.*
hatchet tail. His voice tracks the trail, I
took uncle's airgun from the kitchen
rack found the birds in brash nests
around the back of the sheds &
aimed. *I was triggered by your*
*words urging me to gather shards*
*fallen out of the curved sky.*

55

# Re: phased return

BTW the storms tore away tiles above your room and there was a leak
there left unnoticed while you were away. You'll have to use B29 and
C35 for your lessons tomorrow and until further notice.

Regards, J

Doubtless,
my dreams
will walk me to school,
where I'll watch my breaths in the wind,
and wait for the caretaker to cut sharp keys,
then show me the way to the laboratories.

As he half-waves goodbye,
(barely looking back, before the door cracks shut)
I'll find some wobbly chair, or lean against a workbench,
and learn the space as it stares back at me:
anatomy sets of the unwound brain, the broken down body,
Bunsen burners, crucibles, data loggers, evaporating dishes,
the fume-hood with its seized mouth,
goggles piled in open crates like cast-off clothes,
hot plates (cold), incubators (barren)
jars of drowned toads, fat as dredged-up dead,
kitchen scales, lab coats laid out
longing for an autopsy.

There'll be mortars under nebulae of organic matter,
pebble-smooth pestles, pipettes.
Breezeblocks papered with posters:
<u>quantum theorem</u>, ORGANICS, *orbits*.

Every shelf will emit rubber stoppers or test tubes or utility clamps
and in my frenzy I'll forget where to stack wire gauze
or how to leave the volumetric flasks
because I can't ever recall which the X and which the Y axes
and under the stark strip lights, I'll radiate my ineptitude
and my students will study me from their scientists' stools
glowing like a hole in a restless roof,
as if I'm the kyphotic ape in X-Ray
from the cover of the zoology textbooks
stacked beside the bin.

I dim the phone, switch to airplane mode, hide it behind the books on the bedside cabinet. Later, I'll leave my bed to drop the handset down into the hibernating dark.

# Dandelion

When her hair thinned to furze
we understood her treatment had begun
and warned our classes not to stare
while stunned silver seeds
propagated from her fringe
over her green blazer sleeves
and down onto the roofs of books
in that powdersnow tree pollen
makes when heavy oaks are shook
by sudden storms
for days.

> While they brushed or blew the bracts away
> she perceived gusts from puff-cheeked gods
> blushed until her embarrassment radiated
> like a sharp stain on a clean bed
> so she asked to wear patterned scarves
> in case her friends could see only withered strands
> wound up in sutures as a seedhead
> ruined by the loss of its leaves
> and her neck a pink stem instead
> to be choked
> with cold hands.

> > *Nature tends to sculpt in spheres*
> > said a colleague at a window
> > as we watched crowds drawn near
> > to her as sepals on the back field
> > *cells cluster into colonies around*
> > *centrifuges – cancer galaxies weeds*
> > when it happened despite her mass
> > her absence was an exploding star
> > summoning what mattered only to cast
> > it away like pollen
> > into shade.

# [O TRESPASSIN]

by the time this is read
more of the metal sign
will have disappeared
behind bark in that oak
by the far fence,

        perhaps,

        by then,
the tree itself will be gone,
the whole wood to houses,
or hid in shingle and high tide.
A withdrawal as certain as

        I, you,

        forgetting
that a *no trespassing* notice
was ever hung on that oak,
neglecting how the tree flinched
for a decade then devoted

        a century

        to reclaim it
until the sign said something new
read something else to you, and I,
patient, anonymous offenders
in the glade spent a morning

        before

        returning home
to search photographs online –
burred bikes, burled car parts,
tractors dustbowled in cedars,
gravestones interred in yews –

        pinioned

        to a screen
rendered inert as butterflies.
I withdraw first, then resolve
to forever press non-porous
bodies into the thorax of trees –

        pins, metal signs,

        poems, time –
hoping they store mementos,
like the blackthorn that took

an iron age man before he froze
in the Alps and from his guts
            made a cache
            for ten blue sloes.

# smile

i

*You'd just prefer to stare at your reflection?* he says, finally.
My legs are crossed over the sea wall, my biceps curling
the balustrade so my body padlocks the promenade.
I clench a smile I can't see in our shallow silhouettes
on the approaching tide. There is not enough water yet
to hide our truth but waves black, waves silent, gather up
the four-legged footprints we'd trodden in slow sand.

ii

I thought I could bury you, but each year I remember and it grows inside
me again.

Then I fashion myth out of memory, how we could have gone to a
museum in the city, where you might have revealed a truth I'd known at
some point but forgotten.

*Once statues were sculpted with smiles.*

Then maybe you'd have touched my hand in the empty gallery, perhaps I
would have become porcelain.

*The last memory of a human face should have a smile.*

Then the attendant might have entered through a squeaky door and
you'd release my hand again.

*The world must have become more serious and their problems were reflected
in the art.*

# If one day you woke up and the
# Eiffel Tower was gone

those evenings it balances on the Montparnasse rooftops
from the west windows so you keep them unshuttered
        but make every night moonless from the others,

or how wide roads are so emptied of traffic by its mass
that when rushing from Javel to make the morning train
        its glare can burn as if you've stared at the sun,

and that it is sextant and Polaris both in how it points
every path to itself: the spire, the vaulted space beneath,
        the peddler priests and their plastic reliquary,

how, suddenly, when someone can't see it, it's not because
they're at the prism base looking up through geometric layers
        sky upon iron upon sky upon iron upon sky,

it's because it's gone – the iron that shaped the sky, the light,
the spell – all gone, in no time at all, days, hours even, the city
        would begin the tiny acts of erasure all grievers do:
        understanding the dark; taking detours; forgetting.

In between sleep I used to search the space for you until I found your form everywhere about me. I made your ankles from the spindles at the bed's base, your tendered arm was my headboard, your barrel-body thrust out of the pushed out pillow. If the half-light exposed the lacuna as a dream, I'd turn away from the betrayal and augment you again from a hanging dressing gown.

# dark matter

*I know you: solitary griefs*
                    (Lionel Johnson)

the printers' drawers you kept beside your desk
had been emancipated from a roadside skip

shallow cells that once held typeset were filled
with miniature curios cosseted like gold teeth

our homework one week was to find treasure
an exhibition on our capacity to fill emptiness

soon after your replacement began her post
the cabinet was left outside for the caretaker

I removed one drawer took it home hung it
the blank calendar to a whole winter season

a toppled tower a burnt out apartment block
a hundred opened windows to stare through

I rediscovered mass: feathers acorns blueschist
beech seeds fishing lures pine cones bird eggs

when space becomes a rarity I remodel the cache
keep the meagre language turning in my mouth

I wore the coat with holes in the pockets today
heard dropped pebbles stammer their escape

it is spring I am fluent in a pidgin to survive

this empty space is all that is left of you

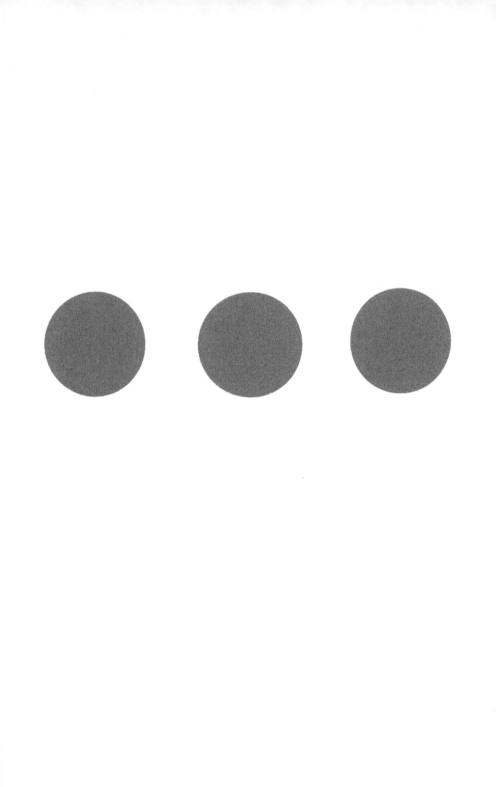

# Afterword

It may read like a legal disclaimer that rises up on the screen immediately after a film, but characters of *In Orbit* are fictional constructs. There is a sense that, in the same way as a narrative voice will, figuratively, have some trace of the poet's accent, the speaker and addressee here probably contain so many fibres of memory that they could almost stand up independently; but, still, they exist, manifest, on paper alone. The deceased teacher is, at most, an amalgamation of different teachers I have known and respected and admired. Maybe they are the teacher who threw beat novels at us when we looked bored, or the teacher who walked across a frozen pond once to make sure he was there for us, or that we were there for him, or the teacher who gave up breaktimes to talk about religions that weren't covered on the syllabus.

I'm starting to unpick that my education and upbringing was more problematic than I acknowledged at the time. For five years in a large high school with only boys on roll, not a single pupil came out as gay. There was an abject terror about being different, and, rather than indulging in what now may be recognised as a natural curiosity of bodies, genders, behaviours, there was a vacuum. This experience may have been purely personal. Others may have had more conviction to ask questions – it's a privilege to be able to go under the radar to avoid bullying – or maybe they had friends, as I have now, who they could explore sexuality and identity with in conversations, in art, in culture. For me, this part of adolescence was more a self-imposed inquisition than inquisitiveness, and, at times, I felt acute shame at not understanding all of my feelings, and repressed every desire to talk about them.

Anyone who's ever seen the film *Dead Poets Society* would want a teacher like John Keating – catalyst, confidante – as a mentor, even if they have to knit that person together from a lifetime of samplers: people, experiences, poems. A large part of this book, I hope, pays homage to the crucial role real educators play in both counselling and inspiring real young adults.

# Notes

## one

'a single atom in an ion trap': the poem features text adapted from the *The New Scientist* online article, 'a single atom is visible to the naked eye in this stunning photo' (Feb, 2018), based on a prize-winning photograph, originally taken by David Nadlinger.

'Cofiwch Dryweryn: 'Remember Tryweryn'' were the words on a mural originally graffitied on the stone wall of a ruined cottage near to where the Tryweryn Valley was flooded by Liverpool City Council in 1960 to create Llyn Celyn reservoir. The wall has been both repeatedly vandalised, repainted, and then reduplicated in multiple sites across Wales. The original mural was painted by Meic Stephens, poet and critic, who was my professor at University of Glamorgan.

'there is no excuse': this poem is based on Shigeru Mizuki's painting of *Gasha-dokuro*, a yokai from Hiroshima Prefecture, depicted as a giant skeleton spawned by the angry spirits of wayfarers who died by the roadside. Mizuki was expected to perform harakiri when he was the only survivor of a bombing attack, but, instead, returned to Japan and learned how to paint with his remaining arm.

'A photocopy sellotaped to a desk – Picking Flowers by Henri Lebasque': there is some ambiguity about the title, and possibly even about this painter, about this artwork. Henri Lebasque painted a similar but separate piece, *Young Girl Picking Flowers*, in 1910, but, despite internet searches seeming to associate him with the painting I'd first seen in a friend's Facebook post, this particular painting may be mistitled, or mis-attributed to Lebasque.

## two

'There's no king of Bardsey Island anymore': the Bardsey Crown is on display in Storiel in Bangor, together with photographs of previous regents of Bardsey Island – an island on the Llyn Peninsula that legend says is home to 20,000 saints – Love Pritchard and John Williams II.

'Instead, I would look at Venus through my telescope': the poem features text borrowed from Brian Cox's BBC episode 'A Moment in the Sun – The Terrestrial Planets'.

'Parallel Circuit': in a parallel circuit, each device is placed in its own separate branch. The presence of branch lines means that there are multiple pathways by which charge can traverse the external circuit. A break in the component will not cause the circuit to cease function.

'Sun, Earth and Moon scale model (Oxford Natural History Museum)': the poem borrows text from a model on the upper gallery of the Natural History Museum, and from the article 'Solving a Celestial Mystery' on the museum's blog, *More than a Dodo*.

'Smoots or': the poem features a line taken from the Fox chapter of *The Book of Trespass* by Nick Hayes.

three

'おもひでぽろぽろ (Only Yesterday)': the poem mentions the pineapple scene from Studio Ghibli's *Only Yesterday*, which can be viewed as a clip on You Tube, and other film streaming sites.

'A photo of the moon shows not a moon but a moon being looked at': the title of this poem is a reference to a quotation by John Berger: 'a drawing of a tree shows not a tree but a tree being looked at'.

'Bird Drawings by CF Tunnicliffe': Charles Tunnicliffe was a painter and illustrator who spent his final years on Malltraeth, Anglesey. His book *Bird Drawings* comprises his self-termed 'feather maps', anatomical paintings of birds. The Tunnicliffe Gallery is part of Oriel Ynys Môn.

'dark matter': this poem was previously published with an epigraph mis-attributed to Robert Frost. The ambiguity may have arisen from the line, originally written by Lionel Johnson in 'The Precept of Silence', being quoted by George Monteiro in his book, *Robert Burns' Poetry of Rural Life* (2014).

# Acknowledgments

I acknowledge that without my wife and son, there would be very little to write about. Without both sets of our parents, and friends, there would be very little time to write. Without understanding headteachers and colleagues, there would be precious little money to write with. Without kind editors and publishers, generous organisers of events, receptive bookshop owners and staff, there would be no place to share writing. And without readers, there would be little function to writing. Thus, I thank all the good fortune that has aligned to create a space, mindset and support network for me to write poetry, and the ambassadors of poetry who advocate new writers, and who are receptive to taking chances with new voices.

In particular, thanks to Amy Wack, with whom a sustained discourse was the initial steps to working with Seren, and to Zoë Brigley and Rhian Edwards, who inherited this project and worked tirelessly to make the book address complicated territories so that an audience comprising all genders and orientations can hopefully read about a love each identifies with in some way. Thanks to Steve McElroy who give the concrete poems their first life in a more ambitious form, and to Jamie Hill, at Seren, for his patience who translated them into arduous typeset, and found a wonderful cover for them to reside in. Thanks to the Mick and Sarah whose care and time transformed a computer file into a book on a library, shop or living room shelf.

The book was partially written during an MA with the Manchester Writing School, so thank you to Andrew McMillan who tutored it as a dissertation project. I have great admiration for the generosity of Chris Meredith and Matthew Francis, tutors from my undergraduate degree, and John Lavin, the Editor of The Lonely Press, who agreed to provide testimonials for the book, and equally for colleagues, friends and family who offered encouragement or reassurance in the years the book came into being. Sincere thanks also to Matthew Haigh, Philip Gross, Mark Pajak and Paul Henry for providing such generous testimonials.

Thank you, finally, to all readers. Although *In Orbit* makes no claim on your experience of grief or your experience of love, I hope you carry the book with you long after you have finished it.